How to use

Feng Shui

to create

Business
Abundance

Keri Norley

Created and published by Keri Norley
© Keri Norley 2015
All rights reserved

ISBN 978-0-9874747-1-1

Thank You

First of all Thank YOU! Thank you for wanting this information and picking up this book and reading it and believing that magic is possible.

Thanks to my mentor Chris Brazel. Without you, this book would not be possible. Your living, breathing love and enthusiasm for this work continues to inspire me.

Thanks to Stacy Kaplan for editing this book with a fine toothed comb.

Thanks to Elle Roberts who put in a crazy, amazing effort to format this book and make it look pretty.

Thanks to all my family, friends, and other mentors for your support and love. There are way too many to mention here, so you know who you are and you rock my world.

And to my boys… My hubby Hugh, and young ones Robbie and Sam. You fill my heart with so much love every day. Without you by my side, encouraging me every step of the way, this book wouldn't be here. I love you as big as all the galaxies.

Foreword

"Clear the clutter in your life and prepare for abundance,"

Paul Maskell.

Life is a journey of abundance if you let it be so.

An abundance of friends, an abundance of peace and tranquillity, an abundance of happiness and yes, even an abundance of wealth.

It has been said that we always end up meeting the people we are supposed to meet, at the time we are supposed to meet them and where we are supposed to meet them.

Does this happen by accident, a chance meeting or a happenstance? Or, are life's fortunate meetings something we draw inexorably towards us? Attract to us if you will? If you stop and think about it, everything on this earth is energy and it has fascinated man for centuries.

Energy powers our homes, our cars, even the waves at the beach. It follows then that energy can power everything that is in and around us in life, even the people we meet and the paths we follow.

As a qualified engineer, I understand energy and I am fully aware of the unseen forces surrounding us, influencing our lives, every single hour of every single day as it has done since the dawn of time. This flow of energy affects our home life, our relationships and yes, even our business lives.

This flow of energy can work to help us, if we let it. Or, it can work against us. I believe it is all about the choices we make. For our actions to create harmony and balance in our lives, we must be conscious of what we are doing . . . every waking hour of every day.

Right down to the simple things like the colours in your home, how your house is set out, the numbers you use throughout your business, even the colour of your underwear can determine your success or otherwise in many ways!

Many a successful person has said, "Whatever you want in life, you can have." However there is a rider to that.

You can have what you want, if you attract the right energy for you.

Feng Shui marries your environment to your life force, and so to achieve your goals you need to arrange your home, your office and your life so energy flows freely. Towards you and around you.

Keri Norley demonstrates this very clearly in this book. And as Keri says herself, she shows you how to:

"Build a pipeline with clients flowing straight towards you."

And you will reap real rewards you never thought possible. So in saying all of this, let me leave you with this one final thought, "you get what you expect out of life" so:

What do you expect out of life for you?

Personally, family, happiness, health, and living a life full of abundance are high on my agenda. Keri's simple explanations and the rituals she writes about in this book will put you well on your way to a balanced environment and a life of abundance.

Yours in future profits,

Paul Maskell
Also known as Clancy of the Information Overflow

Note

Paul has over 150 websites and makes high 6 figures every month all while only working on his business a couple hours a day. The man knows how to attract abundance and manage his energy!

Contents

Who Can Use Feng Shui?

I have written this book with you in mind. This content is for you if you want to super charge your business with minimal outlay and effort.

Read this carefully, because this sort of phenomenal abundance in business is not for everyone. Imagine learning the one secret to building your business that had you only learned it sooner would have catapulted your business growth . . . . The gap between where you are right now and the abundance you want to attract into your life is a tiny fraction and shift in understanding of what you think is possible.

I'm sure you're a busy person with little time on your hands, so I'll get straight to the point: Feng Shui is a system you can learn like any other – you can use it to lift you and your business to whole new levels of personal success and financial rewards. It is a journey that many others have proven really works. It will work for you too – especially if you know the importance of manifesting your own success. How do you begin this shift in your life?

By investing in yourself, starting with your uncompromising belief in your own potential for success. By demonstrating your commitment to that belief with TAKING ACTION.

If this is something you want, then keep reading. Do not waste another minute wishing for abundance – make it happen. You have started a business, so you are already dynamic. Harness that energy and get it all flowing the right way; abundantly. Into your business and into your life.

Flow is a key component of Feng Shui. Getting positive energy flowing into your life in the way that you want requires shifts, but these shifts do not have to be large. Changing small things makes a big difference to the abundance you attract into your business – and in to the rest of your life. It is this dynamic energy that will bring the right changes to your business – and the shifts will be ongoing.

Feng Shui is a living system and it changes with your own transformations. To create a constant flow of abundance into your business you need to pay attention to the signs around you and perform multiple tweaks here and there that will make all the difference to your life. These changes begin with your business environment – and they tend to have excellent flow-on effects to your mindset and emotional wellbeing as well. Nurturing the positivity of the energy flows around you will pay huge dividends.

Want to know one of the best kept Feng Shui secrets around? Here goes: It's not that hard to do!

I want to give you this example right now because it is recent, it is real, and it shows you the power of Feng Shui.

This is just one of my favourite case studies for using Feng Shui to attract abundance to business:

Story

Susan was working on her business, bringing in good money. She had already earned herself a Mercedes 4WD from the company she was working with. She had a team, and they were good, but they were not her dream team. She had a vision board of the team she wanted to work with in building her business, but when she looked at the people they were not anything to dream about either.

I suggested she get rid of the images on her vision board. That's right, I insisted she chuck them. All except the one exceptional team member – we left her on the board. She also found other images that represented what her dream team member would be for her.

We also de-cluttered her work area and threw out a lot of things she did not need. This created space – yes, space for the right energies and the right team members to arrive in her business and guess what? They did, and within the month.

She brought on a team leader that created beyond what most people create in months in her first month on the team. She also brought on a couple other star players within the month.

This qualified her to take a trip to Fiji with her whole family. Something she had only been dreaming about, weeks before.

The changes were simple, small – and monumentally effective.

I want to make 3 things very clear:
1.   I do not possess any supernatural powers. . . if I can do this, you sure can.
2.   This is a systematic process that ANYONE can follow.
3.   Feng Shui just flat out works.

In this book you will learn:
*   How you can attract abundance to your business quickly and easily.
*   The enormous benefits of making small changes to your business environment.
*   The easiest, simplest ways to address any issues of scarcity in your business, with the power of Feng Shui.

The content contained in this book is the culmination of the skills and knowledge I have built up over the past ten years. It is packed with information you can apply quickly and easily in your business.

I know what it's like to hear someone tell you they have exactly what you need to boost your business into the stratosphere if only you can come up with a few thousand dollars. The truth is, I'm not a fan of charging inflated amounts for Feng Shui consults, or building something up to an absurd value. I want to ensure my information is accessible to forward thinking business owners just like you.

The secret here is that Feng Shui is a system we can implement together. You don't just stand back and let me do all the work. It is about the flow of energy – and the energy in your business comes from just one place; that's right – it flows from you, not from me, or from anyone or anywhere else.

This is about what you can attract to your life; your power to make things happen in your business. This book will offer actions that are your actions to take, as you move towards the magnificent future you are creating.

Let's get to work!

The Power of Feng Shui

I am so excited and honoured you are reading this book. You have already taken your first step to creating magic in your life, taking action is how magic happens!

I have been coaching people for around a decade in life, health, business, marketing, and personal relationships. I use all sorts of tools to achieve great results with my clients. When I discovered Feng Shui, it was a game changer.

Even billionaires like Donald Trump and Bill Gates use this magic. Donald Trump said, "I don't have to believe in Feng Shui. I do it because it makes me money." Trump applied the Feng Shui principles to his Trump Tower building in New York so that he could increase his prosperity and success. So if these billionaires use it to help them increase their wealth, you may want to take notes or grab a highlighter to mark up the pages of this book. If it works for them, it can certainly work for you.

Once I began using Feng Shui, I noticed results that used to take months for my clients, started happening in weeks, days, and even hours. It still blows my mind every time I have clients tell me their results, even though I have the most incredible belief that this stuff works.

When I sat down to write this book, I did it with time poor business owners like you – and me – in mind. I could have written a book with lots of small details explaining all the Feng Shui history and getting into minutiae that, quite frankly, is not important for you to know in order to have Feng Shui work for you. That is what this is all about. Simple changes you can make to get abundance working for you now in your business and in your life.

This book has all the basics you need to get results without the waffle and fluff. It is seriously packed full of tips and tools to create abundance in your life. Think of it as a "cheat sheet" for your first steps to creating abundance in your world. If you want to start learning about Feng Shui in detail, there are books for that. This is not one of them.

As a busy mother of two young boys who runs her own business, writes, does Feng Shui consults, coaches other business people, etc., I don't have loads of hours in a day to sit and read. I know most of you are a bit like me and need to make every minute of your day count.

I truly want to get these tools into as many people's lives as possible. It is my mission to help heal this planet, and in order to do that, YOU have to be able to get the information you need. So please use this information with honour and respect for the work and help me make the world a better place by making your life even better than it already is.

Just reading this book will not make you richer. You do actually have to take steps to make things happen. As long as you are willing to take action, you will see results ike magic. So, get reading and take action right away. Create your abundant world.

Note

Before we get started I want to share with you, I am fully aware that this book is written to grow your business using Feng Shui.

In this book, I refer to your home and office. I say this for two reasons. Firstly, a lot of people are working from home, so that is your office.

Secondly, if you work from an office, restaurant, spa, any building outside of your home, it is important to Feng Shui both of these areas.

Your home also influences your energy towards your abundance in your work.

The Science Behind Feng Shui

Here is the only technical part, and I promise it's short.

What is Feng Shui?

Feng Shui is an ancient Chinese term that literally means "wind" and "water". It is used to symbolise the "harmony" and "balance" of how a human being correlates with his environment. The Feng Shui practice is based on the principle of qi or chi energy, also known as "natural energy,", "energy flow," or "life force" (i.e. the energy that binds the entire Universe together). It is through the qi or chi principle that good energy is established and wealth, health, happiness, and stability are either achieved or restored by most Feng Shui practitioners or believers.

The Origin of Feng Shui

Feng Shui is said to have originated from Chinese astronomy. The earliest dates and practices of Feng Shui existed over 6,000 years ago, when the Chinese used it widely for architectural orientation of their prominent buildings such as palaces and tombs.

To date, Feng Shui is currently practiced to promote wealth, health and stability among individuals and businesses.

How It Works - Feng Shui Fundamentals

Basically, Feng Shui works on the principle of the qi or chi energy. The chi energy is believed by the Chinese to be an invisible force that plays an important role in creating harmony and balance in our daily lives.

Chi energy develops a holistic approach, affecting how we perceive things, how we interact with other people and our surroundings, how we carry out our actions or plans, etc. in a confident and secure direction.

It teaches us to be more intuitive and to recognize the volume or intensity of the energy flow around us and how to make effective use of them.

How Can Feng Shui Help You?

Now that I know about Feng Shui, I would say it is crucial to growing your business and having an abundant life. Imagine you had two ways to travel to work; one filled with roadblocks that you had to navigate, and one a flowing stream of traffic. Which would you choose? The easy flowing path, right?

When you use Feng Shui, you create an easy flowing path for the dreams and desires that you want coming to you. It's really that simple. So, unless you like to make life harder than it has to be, use Feng Shui to create a flowing energy or path for good things to come your way.

Simplifying Feng Shui - What You Really Need To Know

There are messages in everything around you. Everywhere you look, there are signs. It's not just the easy to see stuff like billboards and radio announcements either; memos from the Universe are being sent and received all the time on a subconscious level between people, objects, and even the environment.

For years I worked with clients' mindsets to overcome mental blocks and self-sabotage. When I learned about Feng Shui it was like magic to me. People can hide in their own minds and decide what they want to share, but when I step into your home or office, you can no longer hide. Every piece of furniture, art and even the mess shares a message about you, and the most important messages you send and receive are those that tell the Universe what you are up to – and those that tell yourself what you are about. This is the secret to attracting the right kind of energy into your business; you need to send the right messages about what you want to achieve – and yes, those requirements will change over time. They are supposed to. No one – and nothing – in the Universe is, or should be, static. Everything is changing all the time – and a lot of the energy flows in the world come from this very fact of constant change.

It is crucial for you to be aware of the messages that your home shares. These messages will influence your energy, decisions and actions.

The best thing about Feng Shui is that you don't have to go through a 'process'. There is no unfolding what is in your past, or facing your inner demons. No in-depth soul searching and keeping a dream diary for months on end. Not with Feng Shui.

None of that is necessary. This system has been in play for thousands of years, and doesn't need anything more than for you to believe in it – and act on it. That's it; the whole kit and caboodle. Just move the stuff and change your life. It really is that simple.

For example, on your desk, you may have a picture of yourself, doing something, but you are alone. One message that this picture shares is that you are constantly having to do everything on your own. No one is really supporting you and so you just feel it is easier to do it yourself. Now, replace the picture with one of you with other people and allow your team to form around you and help you!

You may have heard the saying 'the map is not the territory'; this is particularly applicable to Feng Shui because this saying is about perception. By changing your surroundings, you can shift the way you perceive yourself, your office, your business – and the way abundance flows in and around your work.

Personal perceptions are vital because if what you tell yourself about yourself and your business does not marry up and support the results you are aiming to achieve, you will find yourself facing an uphill battle for success. The messages you send yourself are likewise critical to your success. Every time you change or shift something to redirect your flow of abundance, you make a bigger difference to yourself than you probably realise. Sometimes the results you get seem out of proportion to the seemingly minor changes you have made – but that is part of the magic too – and part of the amazing power of Feng Shui and shifting your perspective.

When you change your perceptions, you also send a message to the Universe. You set yourself up for different – and better – results.

Shifting the energy with Feng Shui is a journey that you can go on forever. It's not something you do once and never touch again. As your life changes and your desires change, the energy of your home and office must change to attract what you want. You won't want the same things all the time – your wants, needs and desires are changing all the time. Change has an energy of its own as well – and there is dynamism and power in that energy field as well.

Note

I talk about "Universe" in this book. You can call it whatever you like, but what I'm talking about is that something bigger than us that is out there. Some call it God, or spirit. Please feel free to mentally insert whatever word works for you when I use "Universe".

Wherever there is energy flow, there is the potential to affect something in your life in another direction. With careful consideration, and the power to learn, apply and act, you can harness these energy flows and bring abundance into your life in more ways than you ever thought of as possible before. This energy is everywhere. It's in the small details and the big things and it is so much fun to play with this magic and see the incredible results that follow.

When Albert Einstein said "The field is the only reality" he was referring to a law of physics that, in general terms, covers the connection between objects. The law states that objects that have once been joined together in any way, will always maintain an invisible energy stream between them – kind of like a friend you never see, but still feel connected to in a meaningful way.

This connected energy is what Einstein meant by 'the field'. What this law means for you is that the connection – or energy flow – is real and undeniable.

Energy flows between people and objects – and that energy flow, once established, remains no matter what. Feng Shui aims to harness and direct these energy flows; to utilise what is already there and keep the positive power flowing for you, instead of against you or, what is often more frustrating to deal with and observe, right past you.

The flow of energy has a resonance, a power, specific to the objects and people in and around this connection. The flows between these objects create a real energy field that has an impact – and that you can use to your advantage if you know how, and if you are aware of it. For example, if you are playing a musical instrument and want to make a B note, you hit a specific key or play a set of strings and you get the vibration of the B note and the air resonates to that note. Another combination of strings or keys makes your A note, etc.

It is the physical energy field that creates a vibration, creating a specific sound that resonates with our eardrums, enters our consciousness, and that we hear and identify as a specific note.

This is how everything around you works. Everything – every object, image, colour, and placement of these things – has a vibrational energy that creates a specific resonance, harmony, feeling, energy . . . . So when you have a specific number of objects, this resonates with a specific vibration. When you put things in your home, they vibrate in a specific way. With your Feng Shui work, we want to create a vibration or energy that is in flow and makes life feel easy.

Phew! That's done. I told you it would be short, didn't I? :-) Let's get stuck into this!

What Does 'Abundance' Mean For You?

As this book is about abundance, it is important to define what abundance means to you, so that you know what you want to attract into your life. Abundance can mean so many different things, so take a moment now to write down what it means to you.

There is no right or wrong here – just clarity.

_____

_____

_____

_____

_____

_____

_____

_____

_____

_____

_____

_____

_____

_____

"People don't buy WHAT you do, people buy WHY you do it". Simon Sinek

A crucial part of growing your business and creating abundance is knowing your "Why?"

Why do you do what you do?

Generally speaking, people do not get into business just to make money, although it is what usually happens once your abundance begins flowing. Everyone gets into business for different reasons. It may be because you love what you do and want to help others; it may be because you want to create a greener, healthier planet and to leave a sustainable footprint. Maybe it's because you love to innovate and create; maybe because the more money you make, the more you can contribute to others in a massive way.

I don't know what drives you, what gets you out of bed every morning, but YOU need to know. As you look to create abundance, you need to remember WHY you are doing it. If you are only thinking about the money, you may be leaving something on the table.

In order to make this process more powerful for yourself and make your business even more successful, take a moment to write down why you are in business. Why do you do what you do? (Please do not be like those other people who just keep reading. Take a moment right now to figure this out. This one piece of insight can change your whole business).

Write down your WHY

_____

_____

_____

_____

_____

_____

_____

_____

_____

_____

_____

_____

_____

_____

_____

_____

_____

_____

_____

_____

_____

_____

_____

In all the years I have been teaching this, I have looked at knowing your 'why' for two reasons:

1.   Part of attracting good and wealth into your life is showing the Universe that you will be responsible with whatever you attract. If you use your abundance to spread 'goodness' throughout the Universe, then the Universe will want to give you more.

For example, let's look at two friends. One of them would be there for you in a second, brings dinner when you are sick, picks up the kids from school when you are running late, and is a shoulder to cry on whenever you need it. The other is fun to go out with, but always has excuses as to why she cannot help, is always sick, you are always taking her kids, and she is fun when you are together, but generally you actually feel drained when you see her. If one day, both of them need your help, which one will you help? The one who drains you or the one who fills you up? Of course, you will help the amazing person who is always helping you!

The same goes for the Universe. And since, generally speaking, your 'why' is bigger than just you and your desire for more "things", it will mean that you are filling up the Universe . . . and the Universe will provide for you. So once you know your 'why', start doing something about it. If it is to give back in a big way, start giving back now. Even if it is only small amounts, start making your deposits already and the Universe will reward you.

2.   The other reason it is important to know your 'why' is because you can use it in your marketing. People will love knowing that although they may be coming to you for yoga or to have a massage (whatever it is for you), ultimately your dream is to create a healthier planet through movement and helping people be happier one

person at a time. Can you see how someone will pick you for a massage over the person down the street because they are attracted to your 'why'? It feels good to them to be a part of giving back too!

If you want to learn more about this, I just learned of a great TED talk by Simon Sinek you can watch that will go into the concept in more depth. http://tinyurl.com/myxqad2

The Basics of Feng Shui

How does Feng Shui work?

One of the most important tools to have in Feng Shui is the Bagua map. This is a map of the flow of energy. It shows you which areas of your home or office are connected to specific areas of your life.

Beyond the Bagua map, Feng Shui can get very detailed and technical with the cycles of the five elements. There are also magic or lucky charms, corrections for bad Feng Shui, and various other rituals that can all come into play.

Quite a lot of Feng Shui is also just plain common sense; that is just looking at what is around you and seeing what it projects. You will get used to seeing your environment in a whole new way; you will learn to read the signs around you and make the simple – but effective – changes necessary to redirect the energy flows in order to create the most abundance possible for yourself and your business.

You will probably find that you see everything in your world a little differently once you start using some of your Feng Shui skills. You might find you start to look at a lot of the art work and objects that you have all around you.

Like I said earlier, Feng Shui is a journey that goes for life. Once you start to use this powerful tool and see the results, you will want to learn more. Remember, for the purpose of this book, I am going to make everything simple and easy for you to follow so that you can start doing it and see the results straight away.

What kind of results can you expect?

How long is a piece of string? The power of Feng Shui never ceases to amaze me. I am constantly telling people how to shift the energy, what colours to wear, where to move things around, and how to alter the message in their branding. When they make the changes, there is no guarantee as to just exactly what results they may experience, but something magical will happen.

And it is not always what you expect.

Story

Leah and Ron were looking to attract more abundance into their lives. For them, that meant more money. Leah was working long hours in a job where she was undervalued and was unhappy, and Ron was worrying about bringing in enough funds so his wife could take a break from work which no longer inspired her.

We took the mirrors out of their kitchen (if you have any in there, take them out).

The next day, Ron got a call offering him an extra day of contracting work and a big bonus for work he had already done!

They also painted their entry way a new bright lime green colour to bring in new beginnings and Leah was offered a new job in a place where she is super valued.

She also negotiated to have hours that also gave her time to work on her own business as well. And a big bonus – she now works only a short distance from home so she could spend more time with her husband.

Nice results, if you ask me.

When you start playing with all these great tips that I am about to give you my suggestion is that you do not do everything at once. If you take your time to go through the tips, you will see how doing one thing created a certain result.

You also have to be aware and pay attention to the signs. It may be that over the next couple of days you run into 3 different people who all suggest something very similar and if you are not paying attention, you could miss the sign. But if you just be aware and listen to what people say, the billboard or magazine headlines you see, the animals that appear – they are all delivering messages to you. It could be as simple as that, or it could be that as you are doing the tip, the phone rings and a new client books in.

I have seen it all.

Story

Another client, Laura, was looking for clarity around a work situation. She was unhappy in her job, and yet concerned about her job security.

I told her to wear yellow underwear and yellow anywhere else she could get it. The next day, she lost her job.

It was not the result we were expecting, but it was the answer she was looking for and she was able to move forward in ways that she could not have with that job.

She moved to the country for a few months and took some time out. She took care of some health issues while she was away and is starting her new business.

Remember, everything in life happens for a reason, so even though losing her job did not seem like a good answer in the moment, in the scheme of her life it was exactly what needed to happen.

The most important part about playing with Feng Shui is to be open minded, get excited about the possibilities and have fun!

The Bagua Map

Abundance	Fame	Relationships
Health & Family	CHI	Creativity
Knowledge & Belief	Career	Helpful people & Travel

In the interests of keeping my word and keeping this as simple as possible, I am not going to get into all the intricacies of the Bagua map as we are only talking about abundance. So all that you need to know for this part of Feng Shui is that in the far left hand corner (from the entrance, desk chair, driveway, etc.) of every area you work with is the abundance corner.

So if you are looking at your block of land, it is the back left corner of your property. If you are looking at your home or office, when you walk in the front door (not the door you may always use, but the designated front door) of your space, it is in the far left corner. If you are looking at a room in your home, when you walk in the door, it is in the far left corner. Are you following me?

No matter the space you want to shift the energy in to create abundance, always look at the far left corner.

This can apply to desks, counter tops, hallway cabinets, etc.

I will add one tricky little component here. The abundance corner is the far left from wherever the entryway is. If you have a door on the left wall and there is no room to the left of it, then you have no abundance corner for that "entry". So, if your front door is on the far left corner of your home or office and there is no space next to it, there is no abundance corner in your home or office.

Have no fear though; you are likely to have a room that has an abundance corner to work with. Just start looking at the doorways of the other rooms in your house or office and see which rooms have an abundance corner to work with.

You can also use the abundance magic in other areas of your home. It is most powerful in the abundance corner of your home.

Technical Note

If you start to do a bit of Googling on Feng Shui and the Bagua map, you may read about using a compass. There are a couple different theories about Feng Shui and ways to do it. I learned to do it without a compass, which makes my very directionally challenged self happy! It works without a compass, so no need to go confusing yourself and making things more complicated than they need to be.

The easier this is, the more likely you are to do it and get the results you are after in your business.

If you want to further explore Feng Shui and get a deeper understanding of it and how to use the Bagua map take a look at my online program:
www.kerinorley.com/manifestingabundance

Amongst many other things, there is a video on using the Bagua map with even more remedies to help you create better Feng Shui that is about 18 minutes long.

There is another video on general Feng Shui that goes for over 11 minutes.

Awesome stuff, right?!

Setting Your Intention

Before you go and move or do anything with Feng Shui, it is crucial to set your intention. How can you know what you are going to get back from your changes if you do not ask for precisely what it is that you want?

So, let's say you have a dripping tap that needs fixing. Before you fix the tap, you may think to yourself: "I'm stopping any drainage from my finances." While you fix it, you may even think about places that money is leaking out.

Example

> We had a tap that kept leaking and at the same time, I had a monthly subscription to something that I was never using. It was only $14.95/month, but it was wasted money because I didn't use the service. I kept forgetting to shut it off and the tap kept leaking, until I remembered to stop the service. Get what I'm saying?

It could also be that while you are clearing out any dried plants from your house, you set the intention to let go of something from the past holding you back. You may or may not know what that is, so let it bubble to the surface or just pay attention to the signs.

I was once doing some weeding and my intention was to get rid of the "weedy" people in my life. The ones who were not filling me up, so that I had room to let ones in that would be on my journey with me and support me.

At the gym, there were a lot of friendly people who often "dumped" their problems on me. Being a coach and that kind of person, I listened and often suggested ways to help. But when it was my turn to talk about things happening in my world, they would get up to leave. These people often consumed my thoughts and my heart really went out to them.

I turned up at the gym the day after doing my weeding and it was like a lightbulb went on and I realized that these people were not going to be the people who would support me to live my dreams. It was weird, I did not often see them there all at the same time, but that morning, they were all there.

After that day, I somehow saw them less and less and even when I did see them, we often just did not have time to stop and talk.

The weeds were pulled out and I have since created some other amazing, supportive relationships. It was a clearing out of sorts.

Let's Clear Out Your Clutter

The first thing you want to do is clear out the space of the abundance corner.

Really, it does not matter what space, you want to make sure that your home and office are clear of clutter. This may seem like a hard and daunting task, but really the payoff is great. Find ways to 'organise' your mess and reduce clutter.

It is bad Feng Shui to work in a mess.

Everything that is out on display should have a purpose for being there. If it does not, get rid of it. I know that sounds harsh, but you are here to create abundance, aren't you?

Not only is it bad Feng Shui, physical clutter lying around also clutters up your mind. If you want to grow your business and make more money, you need to have a clear head to create, process, attract, see, and visualise new things into your world.

So if you are a hoarder or you love to collect every sentimental item in your life, or you feel bad getting rid of that gift that someone gave you years ago that you never really liked or used, it's time to dig deep and start clearing it out. It's not to say that sentimental things don't have a place, but if they are taking over your space, they need to be put away.

If you are a person who has a lot of clutter and this task feels impossible, I suggest looking for a local professional organiser. These amazing people will come into your home and help you go through everything, find a spot for things and create space out of areas you did not even know existed.

These people can be invaluable. In Australia, check out the Australian Association of Professional Organisers to find a great person to help you. I'm sure there is an equal to this organisation in many other countries or just Google 'professional organiser' to find someone to help!

Tip

If you are really feeling horrible about throwing things out or giving them away, pack them up into a box and store them away. If you can see how much better your life is without the "stuff" and want to get rid of it, then go ahead and wait. Every person I have worked with has felt so good about the changes, they do not put the clutter back. Sometimes though, it takes baby steps, if that is what feels better for you then do it that way. Either way, just do it.

More General Feng Shui Tips

Throw out the Rubbish

Make sure that if anything breaks, either you fix it right away, or you throw it out!

Dripping Taps

Fix Dripping taps as soon as possible. These are a sign of drainage, if there is a leak in your abundance corner, it likely means you are draining yourself of money unnecessarily. You will find more bills coming in than usual. Fix the leak to stop the financial drainage.

Mould and Damp

Clean mould and damp areas. These damp spots will disrupt the flow of clear, clean energy through your home and office.

Plants

Dried plants, spiky plants, and cactii are bad Feng Shui. The points on them create a bad energy. You want to use plants that have round leaves.

Dried plants are like you are hanging onto the past. Get rid of them and move forward.

Empty Vessels

Don't keep empty pots, containers or bottles around you. Many people keep wine or beer bottles they once drank from, or they have empty vases, or empty decorative dishes/platters left around the house/office or on shelves.

This is bad Feng Shui. It leaves a feeling of lack. Anything that is on display should have something in it.

If it's an empty bottle from which you have already drank, I recommend throwing it away. If it's a vase, fill it with flowers or put it in a cupboard. If you fill your vase with flowers, make sure they are fresh ones.

Putting these empty items up high, means you are asking for an empty future. Objects that are high up are about your future.

Plastic

If you use plastic or silk flowers, they are not real. This can imply that your abundance is a bit "plastic" too. Try and reduce the other plastic items around your house for the same reason.

To embrace more Feng Shui goodness check out
www.kerinorley.com/manifestingabundance

What Goes in Your Abundance Corner?

Your abundance corner is the far left corner of your home, office, block of land, etc.

You want to make sure it's all cleared of clutter and feels open and clean.

Before putting these items in the corner, remember to set your intention about what the purpose is for you to use these lucky items.

Then, allow the space for abundance to flow.

Goldfish

Goldfish are very lucky in Feng Shui, especially for bringing in abundance.

It is ideal if you have a fish tank with a filter creating movement in the water, but just having a bowl with gold fish is great too.

You should always have 3, 6 or 9 goldfish in your tank. If you have 9 goldfish, one of them should be black. If you get a fish tank, make sure that you do not put it in your kitchen (even if it is in the abundance corner, just put it somewhere else).

If you have ever had fish, you would know they can have a short life span. My mentor taught me that fish can often take on the negative energy of the space.

So when my fish die, I take it as a sign that something is not working, there is some negative energy that needs to move.

I thank the fish for the sign and then look at my life and my surroundings and think about what it could be showing me and then make changes accordingly. I have such gratitude for my fish.

And one more thing about fish… don't put them in your kitchen.

Citrine

Jade

Crystals

Crystals have beautiful healing and energetic properties. They are such powerful tools to work with. If you haven't ever used crystals, remain open-minded to this idea and be willing to give it a go.

Citrine is my favorite crystal to bring in abundance. It helps with manifestation and attracting wealth, prosperity, and success. It helps with creativity, concentration and increasing energy.

Jade is a beautiful crystal to work with for abundance. It helps to attract good luck and fortune. It helps you connect with your heart and helps you to become who you really are.

Lucky Cats

You have probably seen these in shops by the cash register. They are meant to be placed in pairs and each with one paw raised to attract good fortune and long life. You can place them at a register or in your abundance corner.

Fruit trees

Fruit trees or pictures of fruit are great in your abundance corner, as they signify abundance and prosperity.

If your abundance corner is in your bedroom, don't put the fruit tree or image of it in your bedroom. Use a different abundance corner in your home for this tip.

Water pictures

Pictures of water are great. The pictures must have FLOWING water and the water must be flowing into the abundance area. If the water is stagnant then your finances might be too. If the picture has the water flowing outwards, then it would show that so is your money!

You may be making it, but as quickly as it comes in, it flows out. So move it so that you have the water flowing in towards you.

Lucky Charms

When using lucky charms, do what feels right for you. You don't have to use them all. You may choose to start with ones that match the decor of your home or office.

Chinese Coins

People often ask me about these. Chinese coins represent the powerful union of heaven and earth. They are often used in different ways to bring in good abundant energy. The red string that is often attached to these is what breathes "life" into them and helps to bring in prosperity.

The other choice is to go on a search for the originals. And get the original coins, used in the original times with the energy of prosperity carried with them. They are harder to find and can be more expensive. Both are good and it is your choice. The more you look into the coins the more you will see different ways that they can be used. Some will have 9 coins, each one being a coin from different prosperous dynasties. This will imply that you have the luck and support of the emperors with you.

You can also get one with 3 coins put together and hang it on your doorway in your home (in the inside of your house). This helps bring in abundance. The coins should be knotted in place with red string.

You can also put the 3 coins into your cash box or register, computer, order books, or wallet: Places to which you want to bring a flow of money.

Make sure that you put the coins with the yang side up. The yang side is the one with four Chinese characters. (As shown in this picture).

This is such a great, easy, inexpensive tool to help create more abundance in your world.

It is good to give coins a clean before using them. Also clean them at the beginning of the year to start the year fresh.

Merchant Ship

Imagine that this ship is bringing in your cargo and with it, your abundance. You can place this on your desk, facing towards you so that it is carrying in your abundance. It does not have to go on your desk; it can go in your foyer in an office, but again, make sure that it is facing inwards.

Also, when getting this ship make sure you get a sailing ship, not a war ship with cannons or guns or anything. You want to bring in good luck and fortune, not discord.

In Australia, we have gold coins, so for Aussies it is best to use gold coins to fill up your ship. If you are not Australian and do not have gold coins, just use higher valued coins. No pennies please, remember – you are creating abundance. The other thing you can fill your ship with is gold ingots.

They are another Feng Shui tool and also pretty inexpensive. These represent abundance too, so are a great thing with which to fill your ship. The reason I suggest money as well, is because you are likely to have some coins around that you can put in there immediately, so do not wait and delay your luck.

Three legged toad or money toad

These are great symbols for abundance. Most include a toad sitting on a pile of money, but it will always have a coin in its mouth.

You can have a few of these in your home. Make sure that any multiples in your house are placed discreetly. You do not want it to feel like you are begging and desperate for abundance.

One can be placed diagonally from your entry door, looking at the door. I also rotate one on our desks. They do not belong in bedrooms or your kitchen.

Chinese Jade Plant

These can also be called money plants. Put them in the front door of your home or business to bring in abundance. They should never go out the back, as this will symbolise you sending your money luck out the back door.

Branches of jade plants can be broken off and given to others. This is good luck too. The more you give, the more you receive.

Lucky Bamboo

When you buy lucky bamboo, be mindful of what you get. There should be 3 sticks and they can be in either water or dirt. I am finding that many of the ones that are sold pre-planted only have two sticks and they have no room to move or grow. They are also buried in rocks. This stifles the growth of the lucky bamboo and of course, your wealth.

I have bought my bamboo individually and put them into a small vase that holds them securely. They are in water and you can put just a few stones at the bottom to give them some stability, but do not fill it all the way to the top and trap them.

If you grow them directly in the water, do not throw away the water, just re-fill it when it needs more water.

Lucky Red Envelopes

You can put these in your wallet, cash register, or bank books. Inside the envelope place either a set of three Chinese coins tied in red and gold ribbon or three $2 coins (for the Aussies).

With both these and your Chinese coins, it is good to give them a clean before using them. Then take them out at the beginning of the year and cleanse them again to start the year fresh.

Gold Nuggets

I keep a container of gold nuggets next to my bed so that one of the first things I see in the morning and last before I go to bed reminds me of my abundance. They are just some stones painted gold. Make sure that you fill the container right to the top so that it is abundantly full of gold. And do not use a plastic container.

Tortoise

The tortoise can be used for protection and to bring in good fortune. A good place to put them is at the back door or facing the front door.

Objects To Bring Abundance To You

Make sure that you put a bowl of fresh fruit or fresh flowers on your dining room table. Putting oranges there is great as the orange represents gold.

Putting something abundant there implies that you are creating your abundance and there is always enough.

If you can get a mirror on the wall to reflect your dining room table, that will double your abundance.

Note

> Do not go too crazy on mirrors. Mirrors double whatever they reflect, so make sure you are mindful of where you put them.

Also be sure to keep enough food in your house that you could always cook food if you have people come over.

You feel abundant as you always know that you have food to eat.

Daily Rituals

Goal setting

One thing all successful entrepreneurs have in common is that they write out their goals daily. It does not have to be a long list of 30 goals; just your top goals. The point of this is always to keep them at the forefront of your mind and keep you on task. It is important that you are always prioritising what you do in your day according to achieving your goals.

So start your day by writing out your goals.

Want to know a secret way to write goals so they actually happen?
Try this acronym: SMART goals

S - Specific
M - Measurable
A - Achievable
R - Realistic
T - Timely

Specific

Be specific in what you ask for.

Measurable

Give it a specific number so you know when it happens. e.g.: I will sell 1000 books by… I will have 10 new clients by…

Achievable

Make it achievable. Break down a financial goal into steps. e.g.: You want to make $10,000/month. What products/services do you have to sell to make that happen? It is best to create goal around selling those services vs making the money. The money is just what will happen when you offer an amazing product or service. It is easier to focus on selling that product or service than being lost in the number.

Realistic

It is good to stretch yourself, but make sure you are not being crazy. For example, If you are making $5000/month, don't say that by the end of the year I will be making $500,000/year unless you have an actionable plan that will get you there.

Timely

Give yourself a time in which you want to have reached your goal.

What this means is that you need to make sure that you ask for exactly what you want.

You could write a goal like this:

I want to make $6300/month. This has a lot of missing pieces.

In your business it could look something more like this:

By January 8, 2015 I will have launched my online 6 week DIY Feng Shui program and have 21 people enrolled at a price of $300 per person.

See how specific that is? I know exactly what program I am talking about. I will know that it has happened when I have 21 people enrolled at $300 per person. It is totally achievable for me and very realistic that I can do that. And at the end of the day I know how I will make that money. It is much clearer than saying that I want a financial number but have no idea how it will manifest itself, because I do not have the product or service to back up the goal or desired outcome.

Some people will take time at the beginning of their week to write out weekly goals.

I always have a look at my week and see what I need to do that week in order to get myself closer to my goals. Then I make sure to block out time to get those pieces happening.

For example, when I am creating content. I know that it takes me time to get into the flow and I need time to write. I make sure to block out big chunks of time to create content when I know I will not be interrupted. Then I make sure to totally unplug and not let distractions get in my way. It's an appointment I keep with myself.

Make sure that you know what your goals are, that they are clear and concise, that they stay in the front of your mind and that you are doing things daily to work towards them.

Setting Your Daily Intention

You can do this one of two ways. Both work and both get your mindset in order!

When I wake in the morning, I set an intention for the kind of day I am going to have. I think about what I have going on that day and then get clear on the outcome I want to create, the state I want to be in, and personally - then I dress accordingly.

Something I have not talked about much in this book is the impact of colour on our lives. So, when I set my intention, which is often to gain clarity around a certain issue in my world, I will also put on yellow underwear or clothes to cement my intention for the day. Yellow is about clarity.

But for now, just focus on setting your intention. It can be as simple as smiling as often as possible or truly listening to people today or remaining present to the moment.

You can choose whatever you feel is right for you on the day.

Once you have written your goals out for the day, set the intention of the ONE thing you want to focus on and complete for the day.

Often times we try and bite off more than we can chew in a day. It can often feel so overwhelming that you don't get even the one thing that you could have done, then when you complete it you feel a sense of accomplishment. That is much better than trying to do everything and not completing anything, then beating yourself up for being unproductive.

You may find that you get the one thing done, and then you can move onto another. Just start with the intention to get one big thing done and focus on that and do it well. Then move on if you have time.

If you want to learn more about the meaning of colours check out my Abundance Journal at

www.kerinorley.com/dailyjournal

Honour Yourself

This learning takes time to integrate, but it is important to your success. I remember once hearing someone talk about the Dalai Lama. When he was asked what he does when he is really busy, he said, "I meditate more". When I first heard this, I thought 'That sounds nice, but really that's impossible for us mere mortals.'

And over the years, I have started to embrace and figure out what he means. Often times, when we are stressed, tired, and overworked, it takes us twice as long to do something than it would take if we were fresh and feeling healthy and full of energy. It is far more productive to take some time to "chill out" and regroup then it is to power on when you are stressed, exhausted, frantic.

I embrace this concept. When I feel super busy and really stressed, those are the days I will take an extra few minutes at the beginning of my day to sit in silence, meditate and stare at the ocean; whatever I need on the day. Instead of working like crazy, I take time to sit outside and have lunch in the sun. It is really important to take time to honour yourself and give yourself time and space to just be.

It is amazing how much more focused and productive I am from doing what the Dalai Lama says, and creating space or "meditating more".

Not only that, I feel so much less stressed, so much less moody, and so much happier and at peace with my world. It's one of the best pieces of advice I ever took on board. I highly recommend you work on this, no matter how much you may try and fight it or make up excuses as to why you cannot do it.

Get over it and just create the space. You will thank yourself!

Honouring yourself is also about listening to yourself. You know those voices in your head that say 'Stop! You need a break' OR 'Don't eat that, you'll crash'? Whatever those voices tell you, start listening and following through. They are speaking to you for a reason.

Note

Listen to these voices if you know what they are telling you is good for you, others and the world. If the voices tell you to eat
7 packets of cookies, you may want to rethink.
I'm sure you get what I'm saying here.

Your Money Dance

This ritual is one I learned from Clancy, the great guy who wrote the Forward for this book. I don't know about you, but when a guy who is making high 6 figures a month tells me about a ritual he does every day to feel abundant and create more money in his world, I listen and follow in his footsteps. He has allowed me to share this with you, so take note.

He takes $2000 and dances around with it and sings this "I like money, money likes me, money flows to me easily."

If getting $2000 in cash feels like it is too much for you, start with whatever you can afford to have in cash in your home to dance with. Then increase it as you attract more money. Make sure it is big notes, not $5 bills, so that it feels abundant.

It's pretty easy and simple. It only takes a minute to do and it is powerful! It is just another message to the Universe that you are abundant and you can easily attract money into your world. It works for Clancy!

Remember, it's not just one thing that will bring in abundance. It is about using an abundance of tools to generate your feelings of abundance. You can't get much more authentic than that.

What's Next?

That is up to you. The thing is, believing in yourself will not bring abundance into your life; neither will reading about Feng Shui. The only real way to get abundance flowing into your business is to take action; to gather together all the little bits and pieces you have read about – and do it. Do the things you always said you were going to do. Make those small changes that have massive effects – starting with your business; right now. After all, that is how you can make your dream a reality.

Now that you have some understanding of Feng Shui and how you can apply the principles to your own life, you can get started with your office, or home office. You do not have to do everything you have come across in here. In fact, it's better just to make one change at a time (apart from cleaning your home and/or office). Do one thing differently – do it the Feng Shui way – and see what happens for you. It will be brilliant.

Remember that the energy flows are always there; it is just a matter of harnessing, and directing them, in a way that best serves you and your business. As you have probably gathered already, it is so simple to make one tiny little change – and watch the abundance start flowing into your life.

Choose and change one thing. What will it be? How will it manifest?

That's the really amazing part – magic will flow to you, and you will have caused it.

Who's empowered now? Who's creating abundance now?

Thank you for reading my book – and thank you too, for being proactive. For being dynamic enough not to just buy the book, but also to implement the changes recommended in here.

One of my favorite parts of my work is hearing about people's results. It makes my day and truly lights up my world. As you do the work and see the results, please tell me! Send me an email at keri@kerinorley.com and let me know how this information has rocked your world.

Who is Keri Norley?

With all the stresses that it already takes to run a business, Keri loves helping people to magnify the power of the work they are already doing so that they can fast track getting their dreams and desires to become a reality.

Keri's passion is in helping women to create an energy alignment in their business so that clients, JVs, money, opportunities, etc flow to them with ease. I'm sure you can appreciate what it feels like to "be in flow". Keri teaches conscious ways to create flow and to magnify your abundance in your health, relationships, money and life in general.

Keri has been coaching people internationally to get results in life and business for over 10 years now. She loves helping people expand themselves into being a leader. She believes the world needs a shift in consciousness so that we can make it a better place.

Her mission is to help create more and more leaders to help change the world, because there is so much more power in doing it together.

After getting amazing results with her clients for years using NLP and having a background in health, and the mind-body connection, she has introduced Feng Shui, Colours, Numerology and Shamanism to her tool belt and is currently studying a Diploma in Leadership and Expressive Arts Group Training. These incredibly powerful tools are where so much magic is unlocked.

Our outside world is all a reflection of what is happening inside. And so by very simply moving things around in the outside world, we can shift what happens inside and send a totally different message to the "universe" allowing an amazing flow to happen.

Keri lives in NSW, Australia with her 2 young boys and husband. She is an energetic and engaging speaker, author and facilitator and loves coaching and mentoring her clients to create the life and business of their dreams.

Results from her clients

Keri has one client that was offered a full time job (from contracting work) right after moving just one picture on his wall.

Another client was able to rent out a room in her office that had been empty for a long time within 3 business days of changing a few things in her office space.

One client cleaned a specific set of windows with the intention to get some more clients. Within an hour of doing this, someone called up to book in a group of 6 women for group personal training sessions. What a great way to get 6 new clients. Magic happens!

The work is so fun and her clients love doing their "homeplay" as it feels so good. Really, it's addictive!

The more that Keri's clients do this work, the more they truly step even more into their authentic selves and the more things flow to them with so much ease. So many people say that business is hard. Since bringing these tools into her business, Keri no longer finds business "hard"... It can be so easy when things are set up correctly and they just flow to you.

Keri's Other Products

Numerology Report

Use the ancient wisdom in the numbers to discover even more about your own personality. I also tell you about the numbers in your business. For example: What's the energy behind your website, business name, phone number, bank account detail, etc?

When you know the energy of yourself and your business, you know what's being attracted into your life and business. This is a life changing, thorough report and different than many numerology reports out there. I combine colours, numbers and Feng Shui. So when I share with you some of your personality traits, I'll also show you ways that you can get the most out of your energy through working with crystals, colours, Feng Shui and more.

It is an incredible tool that you can use for life.

www.kerinorley.com/numerologyreport

Manifesting Abundance

This is a 6 module online program that shows you how to go through each room of your home/office and Feng Shui it. Like this book, I leave out all the complicated stuff and give you what you can do that is simple and gets results.
You will not only learn about Feng Shui at a far deeper level, but also crystals, colours, chakras and other mindset "stuff". This program will create some powerful shifts and changes in your world.

www.kerinorley.com/manifestingabundance

Daily Abundance Journal

This little gem should be in the hands of every entrepreneur on the planet. This is to help you stick to the daily rituals of successful people. It's a journal designed to help keep you on track to manifesting your abundance.

If you do not have this amazing tool yet, don't wait another moment.

www.kerinorley.com/dailyjournal

Consulting/Mentoring

If you are interested in having a consult with me for Feng Shui, numerology, or attracting your clients into your business, then please contact me.

keri@kerinorley.com

Let's Make Magic

CPSIA information can be obtained at www.ICGtesting.com
Printed in the USA
BVOW10s1827020316

3898BVAU00001B/1/P